BUCHARE
THREE DAYS

Bucharest gateway, three days in the capital

MICHELLE D BELLIES

Copyright

Table of content

INTRODUCTION
Visit the Palace of the Parliament
Explore the Old Town (Lipscani)
Enjoy Romanian cuisine at a local restaurant
Cultural and Artistic Discoveries
Visit the Village Museum (Muzeul Satului)
Explore the Cotroceni Palace and the Botanical Garden
Attend a performance at the Romanian Athenaeum
Parks and Relaxation
Stroll through Herastrau Park and visit the Village Museum
Explore Carol Park and the National Military Museum
Experience the vibrant nightlife in Bucharest.

INTRODUCTION

A city with a history as rich and varied as the hues of its architecture is located in the center of Eastern Europe. Stories of empires, revolutions, and tenacity abound in this Bucharest, whose cobblestone alleys echo with them.

Empires have come and gone from Bucharest, which was dubbed the "Paris of the East" at its prime. It started off as a little commercial post in the fourteenth century. It developed into a bustling European metropolis with a wide range of influences over the ages. With chapters describing Ottoman control, opulent princely courts, and the turbulent years of communist dominance, the city's history is like an open book.

The first thing that greets you upon entering the city is its architecture. Beautiful Belle Époque façades coexist with elegant neoclassical buildings, and communist-era buildings still retain the scars of a former dictatorship. With its winding, tiny lanes, the Old Town conceals the secrets of centuries-old traders and craftspeople.

However, Bucharest's story is about more than simply the past—it's about a city reinventing itself. There's a real sense of youthful enthusiasm and energy, and the parks and gardens provide a peaceful haven from the bustle of the city.

You are about to go on an adventure right now in the middle of this busy city. A voyage that will take you through a living history, where each turn offers a story to be told, and where Bucharest's own spirit plays a part in a narrative of resiliency, change, and unending cultural diversity. Bucharest is a city eager to share its story with anyone who will listen.Romania's capital city of Bucharest, which is situated in the center of Eastern Europe, is a mesmerizing example of how history and modernity can coexist. Bucharest provides a distinctive fusion of elements, from its medieval origins to the grandeur of Belle époque architecture and the echoes of a past marked by centuries of continuous change

Visit the Palace of the Parliament

The Palace of the Parliament is a colossal structure of great architectural and historical value located in the center of Bucharest, Romania. This magnificent building tells a tale that combines history, politics, and the tenacity of a nation.

The story starts during communist leader Nicolae Ceaușescu's reign in Romania. His idea was to build a monument to Romania's grandeur and power. When work on the palace started in 1984, it quickly became an enormously ambitious undertaking. Ceaușescu's dreams were embodied in the architecture of the palace, which became one of the most grandiose construction projects in history.

The architectural magnificence of the Palace of Parliament is what really makes it unique. It is an architectural wonder composed of almost a million cubic meters of marble, embellished with 3,500 metric tons of crystal, and constructed with hundreds of tons of steel and bronze. With 12 levels, an enormous 365,000 square meter area, and more than 1,000 rooms, the sheer size is astounding.

However, the façade isn't the only thing that catches the eye. You are taken to an extravagant and magnificent world as soon as you enter. A sense of pure elegance permeates the inside thanks to the marble, crystal chandeliers, and elaborate tapestries. Visitors are in awe of spaces like the Union Hall, the Human Rights Hall, and the International Conference Center.

Bucharest's Palace of Parliament assumes a new, alluring charm when the sun sets. The massive exterior of the structure is lit up, creating a warm, golden glow that is visible for kilometers around. Both tourists and residents are drawn to the sight, which fosters a sense of community and shared heritage.

There's a lot going on in the streets around the palace, especially at night. The lively cafes, restaurants, and bars in this region come alive with a delicious blend of international and Romanian delicacies. It's the ideal chance to enjoy regional specialties like sarmale (cabbage rolls) and mămăligă (cornmeal porridge) while thinking back on the grandeur and history of the palace you were just touring.

The Palace of the Parliament is not only a destination for tourists but also a center for various cultural events in Bucharest. Concerts, exhibitions, and conferences are often held within its grand halls, adding a modern layer to the historical significance of the building. These events attract artists, intellectuals, and innovators, fostering a dynamic cultural environment in the heart of the city.

The palace's grandeur and its historical significance are, however, not without controversy. Many Romanians have mixed feelings about it, given its association with the communist regime of Ceaușescu. Its colossal scale and extravagant cost during a time of economic hardship for the nation have left a complex legacy. Yet, this complexity is precisely what makes the palace so intriguing and essential to explore.

In essence, a visit to the Palace of the Parliament in Bucharest is a journey through history and an opportunity to witness the resilience and transformation of a nation. It's a cultural touchstone, a symbol of Romania's past and a celebration of its future. Whether you're drawn to its architectural magnificence, its historical resonance, or its cultural significance, one thing is certain: the palace's story is far from finished, and it continues to captivate the hearts and minds of all who venture within its grand walls.

Explore the Old Town (Lipscani)

There is a location in the center of Bucharest where history can be heard from the cobblestone streets and where every corner is painted with a different tale by the city's architecture. The Old Town of Lipscani, which serves as a living history museum for the city, is located here.

The history of Lipscani dates back to the fifteenth century, when it was a thriving commercial area that drew traders from Leipzig and other nearby cities. You're surrounded by centuries-old structures as you meander through its narrow lanes; these are all reminders of the city's rich past. The bold façades of

Baroque, Neoclassical, and Art Nouveau buildings are covered in elaborate decorations that carry you back in time.

Numerous upscale stores and galleries may be found lining these quaint alleyways. Collectors, fashionistas, and art lovers alike are drawn to the handcrafted gems, antiques, vintage apparel, and modern artwork.

What good is a story without a feast, too? Lipscani is known for its diverse array of eateries and lively cafe culture. Here, you can experience various cuisines and enjoy a drink of Romanian wine in outdoor cafes, or you can enjoy traditional Romanian dishes while sitting in the warm sun.

The city of Lipscani comes alive with nightlife and entertainment as the sun sets. Live music venues, bars, and clubs spring to life, beckoning residents and guests to spend the evening dancing.

You'll find lovely tunnels and hidden courtyards within the maze-like streets. These undiscovered treasures provide serene respites from the busy metropolis.

Additionally, the Old Town has landmarks that enhance the story. The tiny Eastern Orthodox church Stavropoleos Church entices with its exquisite wooden carvings and frescoes. With meticulous restoration, the once-historic Hanul lui Manuc—now a restaurant—retains the vestiges of its past.

Lipscani organizes festivals and cultural activities all year to unite the locals and highlight the inventiveness of the city. But Lipscani is alive with a bustling street life; it's not only about the looks. Every visit to the area is a sensory joy thanks to the district's vibrant environment, which is influenced by street performers, artisans, and sellers. Anyone who wants to discover its stories can easily find Lipscani, which is situated right in the center of Bucharest. This neighborhood is a real-life novel, where the past and present coexist and every cobblestone conceals a mystery just waiting to be discovered.

Discovering Lipscani is much more than just seeing a historic quarter; it's an in-depth look into Bucharest's spirit, a dynamic narrative where each step is a flip of a page showing the dynamic past and present of the city.

Located in the center of Bucharest, Lipscani, also known as the Old Town, is a charming neighborhood where history permeates every cobblestone street and time appears to have stopped. This is a place where every step you take reveals a new chapter in the fascinating story of the city. It begs to be experienced with all of your senses.

The history of Lipscani is as old as the city. Its beginnings can be found in the 15th century, when it flourished as a thriving trading area. Here, traders from

Leipzig and other parts of Europe gathered to exchange goods. You can't help but be mesmerized by the buildings that date back centuries as you walk through the district's winding lanes. These architectural treasures are a blend of styles, including Baroque and From Art Nouveau to Neoclassical, each facade is richly decorated with details that bring the past to life.

However, Lipscani is a vibrant neighborhood rather than just a group of historic structures. Its streets are full of bustle, with a variety of upscale stores and galleries. Antiques, vintage apparel, and one-of-a-kind handcrafted goods are a treasure trove for collectors. Visitors who enjoy art can peruse modern galleries, which showcase the city's vibrant creative scene.

A narrative wouldn't be the same without some delicious food, of course. Old Town draws tourists with its unique mix of restaurants and vibrant cafe culture. Here, you may savor traditional Romanian fare in outdoor cafes while soaking up the sun or explore international cuisines accompanied by a glass of local Romanian wine.As the sun dips below the horizon, Lipscani experiences a breathtaking change. It grows into a hub for nightlife and entertainment. The neighborhood comes alive with its live music venues, bars, and clubs. New experiences and tales are created when locals and visitors come together to dance the night away, eventually becoming part of the district's folklore.

Like well-kept secrets, lovely courtyards and passages can be found nestled within Lipscani's winding streets. These hidden jewels are like a quiet chapter in a story—they provide a moment of peace and quiet from the busy city.

The Old Town is delighted to display important landmarks.Lipscani's Old Town, in the center of Bucharest, is still telling its enthralling story. This district is a living, breathing testimony to the city's past, and it begs you to join in on its ongoing drama as you explore its twisting streets and legendary buildings.

The town of Lipscani has a long history dating back centuries, when it was a thriving hub for tradesmen traveling from

Leipzig throughout Europe. Buildings that depict an architectural journey through the ages line its historic streets. Facades with elaborate embellishments that are Baroque, Neoclassical, and Art Nouveau offer a visual symphony of history. Every structure has a distinct story that it whispers.

This neighborhood is more than just a historical site; it's a location where the old and the new coexist peacefully. There are a ton of unique stores and art galleries in this area. A world of handcrafted treasures, retro clothing, and antique curiosities can engross collectors. Contemporary galleries, which are the beating center of the city's creative scene, will captivate art enthusiasts.

Of all, there should be delicious moments in any interesting story. The Old Town is well known for both its diverse selection of eateries and its lively cafe culture. At outdoor cafes, you can enjoy traditional Romanian cuisine while soaking up the sun, or you can sample cuisine from around the world while sipping on a glass of regional Romanian wine.

Lipscani becomes a world of lively nightlife and entertainment as dusk draws in. Bars, clubs, and live music venues abound in the district, captivating the attention of both locals and tourists. Every night, when people gather to celebrate life, fresh chapters in the story are written here.

The winding lanes are like hidden chapters in the story of the district, with quaint courtyards and alleyways hidden behind them. In the middle of a busy city, these hidden jewels provide brief respites where you can think back on the story you're living.

Among the architectural gems are notable locations that enhance the narrative of the Old Town. The little but lovely Stavropoleos Church invites with its gorgeous wooden carvings and murals. The nearby historic Hanul lui Manuc, which was formerly a well-known inn, has been painstakingly renovated and is currently a restaurant that honors its history.

Lipscani hosts festivals and cultural events all year-round that foster community spirit. These incidents give visitors fresh perspectives and experiences by capturing the district's vibrant and ever-changing character.

However, Lipscani's story would be incomplete without the colorful street life that occurs every day. The district's lively environment is enhanced by street performers, artists, and sellers, making each visit a distinctively participatory experience.

Every step you take in Lipscani, tucked away in the center of Bucharest, seems like you're turning a page in a living book. It is a live, breathing monument to the past and present of the city, not just a historical neighborhood. You immerse yourself in its ever-changing story with each visit, learning about its history, culture, and way of life.

Enjoy Romanian cuisine at a local restaurant

The enticing scents filling the cool evening air în Cluj-Napoca, Romania, enhanced my senses as I walked around the city's cobblestone streets. A quaint restaurant nestled away in a corner caught my eye with its cozy atmosphere and the promise of a real Romanian culinary journey under the gentle glow of lamps.

Because of what locals had told me about Romanian food, which I discovered at this local restaurant, I was curious about this hidden culinary gem. I knew I was going to be in for something unique when I saw the modest wooden door and the hand-painted sign that said "Bucătăria Românească." The warm and welcoming ambiance was created inside by the traditional décor adorning the comfortable space.

I was greeted with a warm smile by the welcoming hostess, who showed me to a rustic wooden table covered in a red and white checkered tablecloth. I was welcomed by a menu that had a wide selection of Romanian delicacies as soon as I took a seat. The options, which ranged from flavorful meats to nourishing soups, were enormous—but in the greatest kind of manner.

I made the decision to begin my culinary adventure with a bowl of tripe soup, known as ciorbă de burtă. When it got to my table, the air was filled with its pungent perfume. The tripe was tender and the broth had a sense of fresh herbiness. The first spoonful showed a blast of flavors. It was a gastronomic symphony that resonated with my palate.

I couldn't help but try mămăligă with sarmale for the main meal. The mămăligă was a hearty, polenta-like porridge made of cornmeal that was topped with a heaping portion of crumbled sheep's cheese and a dollop of sour cream. Next to the mămăligă came the sarmale, which are cabbage rolls filled with a blend of minced beef and pig. This dish's interaction of flavors and textures was superb; the rich, salty sarmale was well counterbalanced by the creamy mămăligă.

Satisfied, I chose to treat myself to a specialty of the area: papanasi. These were warm, fried doughnuts with a drizzle of berry jam and a dollop of sour cream on top. The surface was beautifully crispy and the inside was tender. Every mouthful was a delicious combination of sweet and topped with a drizzle of berry jam and a dollop of sour cream, tender on the inside. Every mouthful was a delicious combination of tart and sweet.

I couldn't help but notice the real kindness of the restaurant workers during my entire meal. They were delighted to impart anecdotes regarding the recipes, customs, and background of Romanian food. Every facet of the eating experience was replete with their obvious enthusiasm for their culinary heritage.

I left the restaurant at the end of the evening, full of food and a happy heart. My experience savoring Romanian food has been enlightening, a flavorful journey, and has strengthened my bond with this stunning nation's culture. The Romanian The discovery of flavors through gastronomy has allowed us a closer understanding of this stunning nation's culture. Romanian food had become ingrained in my soul, and I was certain that I would continue to appreciate its delicious food long after I had left that quaint Cluj-Napoca restaurant.

My exploration of Romanian cuisine was far from over. The following day, I arrived in Bucharest, a busy city renowned for its varied culinary scene and buzzing food markets. I went to a nearby market where stands selling seasonal, fresh produce indicated that I was still on my quest to learn more about Romanian cooking.

Everywhere I looked around the market, I was welcomed by the vivid hues and alluring aromas of fresh local vegetables. Ripe tomatoes, herbaceous herbs, and handcrafted cheeses created a visual feast for the senses. I was given samples of products by amiable merchants, and I couldn't help but sample some local Romanian wines, which were a great match for the food of the nation.

Bringing the flavors of Romania back with me, I picked up supplies to make some of the dishes I had tried at the restaurant in Cluj-Napoca. I bargained for some mămăligă cornmeal, which I discovered was a common ingredient in Romanian homes, as well as a head of cabbage and fresh pork. The vibrant market demonstrated the value of using locally produced, fresh ingredients in Romanian food.

Once I was back in my rented place, I started my own cooking experience. Equipped with a recipe acquired from the eatery, I commenced crafting sarmale. It took some dexterity at first to roll the seasoned meat mixture into the soft cabbage leaves, but I quickly got used to the task's rhythmic pattern.

It required some perseverance to cook the mămăligă to the ideal consistency—thick, creamy, and filling. I was in my kitchen, smelling the cornmeal porridge, and I couldn't help but think of that small eatery in Cluj-Napoca.

as the scent of the porridge made with cornmeal permeated my kitchen.

At last, I felt a sense of success as I served myself a dish of mămăligă and sarmale. I was surprised at how much the dish tasted like the one I had eaten at the restaurant. It served as evidence of how crucial it is to maintain customary cooking practices and culinary history.

But the identity of the papanasi remained a mystery. I tried my hardest, but I was never able to get the precise texture and flavor of those sweets.

Cultural and Artistic Discoveries

The dynamic city of Bucharest is located in the center of Eastern Europe. For those who are willing to explore, the city offers a rich tapestry of creative and cultural discoveries. The capital of Romania, known as "Little Paris," has a rich past that has profoundly influenced its creative and cultural scene.

Bucharest is a living museum of centuries' worth of architectural styles because of its diverse architecture. The cityscape is a visual record of its turbulent past, molded by eras of Ottoman, French, and communist influence. The harsh, functional architecture of the communist era coexists with the grandeur of Belle Époque buildings with their elaborate façade. Every architectural era provides an artistic window into the city's constantly changing identity by reflecting its past, present, and future goals.

The soul-stirring music of Romania captivates everyone strolling through the narrow lanes. The musical landscape of Bucharest is a tasteful fusion of traditional, classical, and modern styles. Romanian folk songs' eerie rhythms and the folklore sounds of the nai flute and cimbalom create a deep connection to the past and customs of the country. Conversely, Bucharest is a veritable paradise for lovers of jazz, with a multitude of venues presenting elite shows that honor the city's unique character.

The city boasts a distinguished literary legacy, having produced renowned authors like George Călinescu, Eugène Ionesco, and Mircea Eliade. Their creative output, which draws from the city's rich cultural diversity and complicated past, reflects the intellectual ferment of the metropolis. A window into this literary past is offered by Bucharest's quaint bookstores, some of which are housed in old buildings. They provide a vast array of books that delve into the depths of Romanian culture as well as the human condition. and the intricacies of Romanian culture.

A stroll through Bucharest's art galleries and museums reveals a treasure trove of artistic expression. The National Museum of Art, residing in the former royal palace, boasts a collection of European paintings that rivals some of the world's most famous art institutions. It is a testament to the enduring power of artistic creativity and the city's deep appreciation for visual art.

It is impossible to talk about Bucharest without talking about its thriving theater culture. There are many different types of theaters in the city, from opulent opera halls to cutting-edge performing venues. The theaters in Bucharest are a reflection of the city's diverse cultural influences; they present a variety of shows, including modern dance, experimental theater, and classical ballet and opera.

Bucharest is a culinary melting pot that combines international influences with Romanian traditions. The city's marketplaces and eateries provide a wide range of gastronomic experiences that highlight regional products and customary cooking techniques. Indulging in the delicious mici (grilled sausages) or mămăligă (cornmeal porridge) with sarmale (cabbage rolls) is not only a culinary adventure but also a cultural investigation of Romania's culinary legacy.

Immersion in Bucharest's creative and cultural riches makes one intensely aware of the city's dynamic and ever-changing nature. Bucharest is a live, breathing city that embraces its history while paving the way for the future. It is not a place stuck in time. The city's artistic aspirations and creative energy are proof of its ability to bounce back from past setbacks and emerge stronger, with a rich cultural identity that never fails to enthrall and inspire visitors.

Furthermore, Bucharest's commitment to inclusiveness and diversity is demonstrated by the city's cultural and artistic scene. Bucharest, situated at the meeting point of Eastern and Western Europe, has become a melting pot of cultural influences, fostering a diverse range of artistic manifestations. Celebrated are the coexistence of many ethnicities and highlights the distinctive ways in which they have enriched the cultural fabric of the city.

Bucharest has embraced street art as a dynamic and colorful medium for artistic expression in recent years. Local and international artists use the city's walls as canvases, utilizing graffiti and murals to express their thoughts, tell tales, and give the city's visual identity a modern twist. These art pieces, which are frequently located in unexpected locations throughout the city, are a testament to Bucharest's dynamic nature and openness to embracing contemporary artistic trends.

Bucharest's numerous festivals and events further demonstrate the city's dedication to fostering variety in culture and the arts. Every year, the world-class George Enescu International Festival honors the well-known Romanian composer and brings together musicians and fans from all over the world. In the meantime, the city's passion for this classic American art form is on display at the International Jazz Festival Bucharest, which brings together enthusiasts and performers for performances that will never be forgotten.

Bucharest's dynamic LGBTQ+ community is an essential component of the city's cultural mosaic. The city proudly promotes LGBTQ+ events, parades, and film festivals every year that encourage diversity and inclusivity. These celebrations of love and human rights are a monument to Bucharest's progressive ideals and dedication to building an inclusive community for all.

Bucharest's dedication to conserving its historical and architectural legacy is apparent amidst these artistic revelations. The Village Museum is an outdoor display that honors the value of preserving cultural legacies by presenting typical village life in Romania. In a similar vein, the enormous architectural marvel that is the Palace of Parliament attests to the city's capacity to transform imposing buildings from its convoluted history into useful modern assets.

The narrative of Bucharest's creative and cultural discovery is one of adaptability and perseverance. It is a story that illustrates how the city has been able to weave together its rich past, varied cultural influences, and dynamic present to create a mosaic of artistic expression. The artistic and cultural riches of Bucharest enthrall tourists as well as create a lasting impression, attesting to the city's continuous development as a vibrant center of Eastern European culture and the arts.

Visit the Village Museum (Muzeul Satului)

The Village Museum, or Muzeul Satului, is a live example of Romania's rich and varied cultural legacy, and it is tucked away in the energetic center of Bucharest. Time seems to stop still at this outdoor museum, also known as the "Dimitrie Gusti National Village Museum," where guests can travel through centuries of rural life, history, and customs.

The instant one enters the vast grounds of the museum, they are taken back in time to a bygone era, where the simplicity and peace of the Romanian countryside prevail over the bustling of modern city life. The Village Museum is a vast 30-acre (12-hectare) area that was painstakingly created to capture the atmosphere of rural Romania. It preserves a way of life that is dying and acts as a window into the past.protecting a dying way of life and demonstrating the Romanian people's resilient character.

The museum's collection of traditional homes and buildings is one of its most alluring aspects. Explore this interesting collection of real homes, farmhouses, churches, water mills, and other structures, each of which represents a distinct area of Romania. It is remarkable how different Romanian communities' cultures, materials, and design sensitivities are reflected in the architecture. The structures have been painstakingly dismantled and neatly reassembled at the museum to capture the spirit of their original sites.

You are astounded at the level of detail in these homes as you look about. The interiors are furnished with antiques and period-appropriate home decor, providing a window into the everyday routines of Romania's rural residents. From the Moldavian shepherds in their quaint huts to the Transylvanian Saxons in their sturdy, fortified mansions, each dwelling offers a close link to the people who once called these walls home.

There are also numerous workshops and exhibitions at the Village Museum. Woodworking, weaving, and ceramics are among the ancient crafts that are continued by skilled artisans who are frequently clad in traditional garb. By seeing these craftsmen in action, visitors can develop an appreciation for the skill and commitment that drive Romania's artisanal traditions. Furthermore, the museum frequently presents cultural activities and shows, such as folk dances and music, which uses the energy of the present to bring the past to life.

The Village Museum's verdant environs further envelop guests in Romania's breathtaking natural splendor. There are meadows, gardens, and orchards scattered across the grounds, all of which are bursting with native vegetation. In the middle of the busy metropolis, tourists can take in the clean air and tranquility of rural landscapes that have been preserved by meandering along trails surrounded by trees.

The Village Museum celebrates Romanian customs, holidays, and rituals all year long with special displays and events. These events give a clearer picture of the nation's cultural fabric and a more profound comprehension of the importance of these traditions in Romanian culture.

More than just a trip down memory lane, a visit to the Village Museum offers a chance to consider the resilience of customs and the value of maintaining a nation's cultural heritage. This open-air museum serves as both a living history archive and a reminder of the Romanian people's resilient spirit. It promotes a connection between tourists and a rich and varied heritage that is as lively as the nation itself.

making it an essential stop for anybody interested in learning more about Romania's diverse cultural heritage. Experiencing the Village Museum is like entering a time machine that takes you back in time to a different Romania. The place's evocative environment evokes a strong sense of nostalgia and respect for the traditions, artistry, and perseverance of the generations who have called these rural houses home.

The Village Museum is a goldmine of information for anybody interested in history and the development of Romanian society. It's clear from meandering around the many structures how rural Romanian life has changed and evolved throughout the ages. The displays at the museum assist visitors in tracking changes in agricultural techniques, architectural styles,sociocultural structures and agricultural methods.

The museum's dedication to authenticity is among its most alluring features. The village atmosphere is kept as close to its former state as possible thanks to the careful preservation and restoration of the buildings and displays. It's a labor of love that represents the commitment of the historians and curators who toil hard to protect the country's cultural legacy.

The Village Museum is a vibrant organization that gives Romanian customs new life rather than just being a collection of old houses. Visitors can immerse themselves in Romania's rich cultural legacy through reenactments of traditional weddings and ceremonies, as well as seasonal activities honoring festivals like Easter and Christmas. It is a place where long-standing customs are revived and Romanian folktales and legends ring true with vibrant color.

The Village Museum offers tourists, families, and students a rich and engaging educational experience. It's a location where learning about the past is made more tangible and immersive than it is in history books. Pupils develop a greater understanding of their own cultural heritage, and foreign guests are given a special perspective on a facet of

Romania that is frequently disregarded in the shadow of its metropolitan attractions.

The Village Museum's appeal is rooted in its ability to provide visitors with a thorough grasp of the cultural continuity that has shaped Romania into what it is today, rather than only a look into the past. Its outdoor classrooms impart timeless teachings about the value of tradition, the tenacity of heritage, and the significance of maintaining the bonds that unite us with our past.

Essentially, a trip to the Village Museum is an exploration of Romania's essence. It's a journey that captures the spirit of rural Romanian customs and offers a priceless window into the history and legacy of the Romanian people. It is a location where history is not lost but rather lives on and inspires us, serving as a constant reminder that the past is, in fact, an essential component of the present and the future.

Explore the Cotroceni Palace and the Botanical Garden

The Cotroceni Palace and the Botanical Garden are two amazing locations in the center of Bucharest that entice visitors looking to learn more about the natural beauty and historical significance of the city. These two discrete locations are cultural treasures that provide special perspectives on the spirit of the Romanian metropolis.

The Presidential Palace, sometimes called the Cotroceni Palace, is a remarkable piece of architecture that has had a profound impact on the history of the nation. You're astounded by the imposing neoclassical style, which combines Italian and French influences, as you get closer to its massive façade. This magnificent building radiates refinement and history with its stately columns and elaborate details.

Constructed as a monastery in the seventeenth century, the Cotroceni Palace was converted into a royal home in the nineteenth century. Currently, the palace functions as the official house of the Romanian President, with guided tours available for the public in select areas. You cannot help but feel as though you have been transported back in time to a time of elegance and monarchy as you explore the sumptuous chambers and galleries.

There's more to the palace than just its architecture. Its walls include a rich tapestry of history and art that is equally enthralling. Take in the intricately painted ceilings, opulent furniture, and magnificent artwork that adorn the palace's interior. It seems as though Romanian history and culture are brought to life.

before your very eyes, providing an opportunity for a deep and meaningful connection with the country's history.

The Bucharest Botanical Garden is a natural refuge in the middle of the busy metropolis, located next to the Cotroceni Palace. Founded in the 19th century, this verdant oasis is home to a wide variety of plant species from all over the world, demonstrating the city's dedication to protecting biodiversity and promoting environmental education.

It is a sensual experience to walk around the garden's trails. A pleasant diversion from city life is provided by the surrounding vegetation as you stroll by shimmering ponds and bubbling brooks. The Botanical Garden is a serene haven of well-kept landscapes, reflective ponds, and a tastefully blended collection of plants from different climates and habitats that showcase the beauty of nature.

The varied plant collections provide witness to the labors of numerous generations of horticulturists and botanists. You'll see colorful flowerbeds, enormous trees, and unusual species that will make you reevaluate how diverse the world's plant life is. With its variety of tropical and subtropical plants, the greenhouse complex is especially captivating, giving guests the opportunity to experience several climates all inside one building.

The Botanical Garden is a haven for plant enthusiasts as well as a center for research and education. It is crucial to the preservation of rare and endangered species and helps scientific efforts to understand and protect the natural environment. Many of the garden's sections are also meant to highlight certain kinds of attractive, medicinal, and agricultural plants, providing useful knowledge about the practical applications of botany.The Cotroceni Palace and the Botanical Garden both represent Bucharest's dual nature, which values the natural environment's beauty and significance as well as its rich historical and cultural past. Taken as a whole, they depict a city committed to preserving its past while also being shaped by it.

The Cotroceni Palace offers tourists a deep understanding of Romania's past through its exquisite architecture and historical significance. You are engulfed in the legends of the kings, queens, and statesmen who have molded the course of the country as you meander around the palace's halls. The beautifully furnished and artfully decorated apartments offer glimpses into a bygone age when the nobility and royalty were integral to the political and cultural life of the city.

The palace's enduring significance in Romanian society today is highlighted by its function as the president's official residence. It is a location where modernity and history meet, illustrating the site's ongoing significance. A trip through time to see the changing tapestry is provided by a visit to the Cotroceni Palace. is a trip through time that allows you to see how Romanian culture and government have changed over time, from its regal history to its current democratic character.

The Bucharest Botanical Garden, on the other hand, provides a cool and instructive diversion from the bustle of the city. You can fully appreciate the richness and beauty of the natural world here. An enthralling variety of flora and landscapes will surround you as you meander through the garden's numerous parts. A haven for those who enjoy the outdoors, the garden features tranquil ponds that reflect the sky and beautiful flower beds that burst with color.

The garden is a haven for those who enjoy the outdoors, with peaceful ponds that reflect the sky.

Beyond its aesthetic value, the Botanical Garden is significant. It functions as a living laboratory where scientists, conservationists, and botanists study, record, and save the world's plant life. The garden has a major educational role as well, since it helps visitors develop a greater respect for the environment and encourages environmental care.

The contrast between these two locations perfectly captures the spirit of Bucharest: a city that values education and conservation while respecting its history and cultural legacy. When visiting these locations, tourists can enjoy Bucharest's peaceful cohabitation of nature, culture, and history. The city is always changing while honoring its past.

Discovering the Botanical Garden and Cotroceni Palace is a fascinating trip that lets you experience Bucharest's essence. It's a chance to discover the city's complex personality, which blends the grandeur of historical landmarks with the serenity of the surrounding scenery. When combined, these locations enhance Bucharest's cultural and sensory offerings, fostering reflection, admiration, and a closer bond with the natural environment and the city's history.

Attend a performance at the Romanian Athenaeum

The Romanian Athenaeum in Bucharest, also known as the "Ateneul Roman," is a tribute to the architectural magnificence and cultural diversity of the city. It's a location where history, architectural genius, and the arts come together to produce an enthralling experience.

The Athenaeum's breathtaking architectural design is immediately apparent. Its elaborately detailed neoclassical façade exudes an air of eternal beauty. Travel brochures and postcards featuring Bucharest's famous dome, embellished with paintings and a magnificent peristyle, have been a feature of the city for many years. The Athenaeum is a cultural treasure, but what's within is even more amazing than its stunning appearance.

There is an air of grandeur as soon as one steps inside the Romanian Athenaeum. A masterpiece of acoustical engineering, the circular music hall is built so that every sound made on stage reaches every corner of the space. An aura of luxury and creative inspiration is created by the elaborate décor, which includes elaborate frescoes, golden accents, and a massive chandelier hanging from the ceiling. In a sense, the Athenaeum is a living artwork, a place where the building is an essential component of the performance.

The Romanian Athenaeum is a cultural landmark of great importance in addition to being a masterwork of architecture. The "George Enescu" Philharmonic, named for the most well-known composer from Romania and one of the most significant artists of the 20th century, calls it home. The Athenaeum's cultural value is enhanced by the presence of this philharmonic orchestra, which frequently presents performances, recitals, and concerts of the highest caliber.

A trip into the core of Romanian culture can be had by attending a performance at the Romanian Athenaeum. It's a chance to take in the elegance and profundity of classical music, a genre that has greatly impacted the artistic legacy of the nation. The chamber pieces, symphonies, and concertos that fill the room are proof of the music's continuing power to Utilizing music to convey human experience and elicit feelings

The importance of the Athenaeum goes beyond classical music. Numerous historical and cultural events, such as significant political assemblies and international conferences, have taken place against this backdrop. Its influence on Romania's development as an artistic and cultural nation is immeasurable.

The Romanian Athenaeum exudes an electrifying atmosphere of awe and eagerness for the musicians and performers. The audience joins the orchestra on stage and as the conductor lifts the baton, they are immersed in a common experience that cuts beyond linguistic and cultural boundaries. At this point, music transcends all languages and takes the listener to a place where words can never fully express the depth of emotion and artistry.

The Romanian Athenaeum is more than just a place to see shows; it's a haven for the arts, a place where the spirit of innovation and human expression is encouraged. It is a place where guests may engage with the creative spirit of Romania and a living testament to the country's cultural legacy. an opportunity to fully engage with the beauty and artistry that characterize Bucharest's cultural environment. It's an encounter that leaves a deep impression, a remembrance of a city that reverently and passionately cherishes the arts.

The significance of the Romanian Athenaeum goes beyond its use as a location for musical events. It has long served as a center for intellectual and cultural pursuits, drawing together notables from a variety of disciplines to celebrate ideas, literature, and the arts. For more than a century, the exchange of ideas and creativity has flourished there.

Bucharest's unwavering dedication to the arts and culture is demonstrated by the Athenaeum. It represents a city that is incredibly proud of preserving and honoring its creative heritage. The Athenaeum is a monument to the value of creating an atmosphere that values creative and intellectual pursuits, even beyond its beauty and aural distinction.

The Romanian Athenaeum's impact extends much beyond the boundaries of its home city. It is a historically significant site that has permanently altered Romanian culture. Romania's artistic greatness is embodied in the music that reverberates from its grand auditorium, captivating listeners domestically and internationally. functioning as a dynamic embodiment of Romania's artistic brilliance.

The Romanian Athenaeum is a source of inspiration, a preserver of customs, and a link to the past. It serves as a point of convergence for Bucharest's historical and current cultural elements, reminding tourists that the city is shaped by both its rich artistic legacy and its contemporary accomplishments.

Experiencing a show at the Romanian Athenaeum is more than simply a night at the opera; it's an opportunity to immerse oneself in the culture and establish a link with the very center of Romania. It is an encounter that captivates the senses, arouses the heart, and leaves a lasting impression on those who have the honor of being in its audience. It is evidence of the arts' continuing ability to inspire, motivate, and bring people together, as well as a reminder that creativity and beauty are universal languages that cut across boundaries and profoundly link people.

Parks and Relaxation

Romania's energetic capital, Bucharest, has many parks and green areas that offer a nice break from the bustle of the city. Within the metropolitan landscape, these peaceful oases provide chances for leisure, recreation, and connecting with nature. They are havens of calm.

One of Bucharest's largest and most well-liked green areas is Herăstrău Park, sometimes known as the "Central Park". Located near Lake Herăstrău, this park spans more than 400 acres and is a verdant haven. Visitors are greeted with a sense of tranquility and natural grandeur as they stroll along its pathways lined with trees. The King Michael I Park, with its opulent Elisabeta

Palace offering an insight into Romania's royal past, is the park's focal point.

The Village Museum (Muzeul Satului) is a must-see location within Herăstrău Park. This outdoor museum showcases real rural homes and buildings while putting guests in the setting of traditional Romanian villages. Discovering the country's cultural legacy in the splendor of nature presents a singular chance.

Carol Park is another jewel in Bucharest's park system, renowned for its magnificent Mausoleum and dramatic panoramas. The park's high position affords expansive views across the city, making it a great place to take in the diversity of Bucharest's architecture and the magnificence of the Palace of Parliament.

In the center of the city, Tineretulu Park has a mix of vegetation, walkways, and lively entertainment spaces. Locals love it for outdoor activities like picnics and leisurely walks. The lake in the middle of the park adds to its charm and offers a serene environment for reflection.

The Bucharest Botanical Garden, a natural sanctuary with an amazing array of plant species, is situated in Herastrău Park. You are exposed to a variety of habitats as you walk around the garden's grounds, from tropical greenhouses to decorative gardens. For those who enjoy botany and the beauty and diversity of nature, the garden is a veritable paradise.

The parks in Bucharest are used all year as locations for artistic and cultural events. These green areas are frequently used for festivals, concerts, and outdoor events. For instance, the lively artistic scene of the city is celebrated at the regular music festivals and cultural events held in Herăstrău Park, which draw in both locals and tourists.

City parks in Bucharest also feature community projects and urban gardens, demonstrating the city's dedication to environmental sustainability. These programs support the growth of regional food and foster a sense of connection among locals.

However, leisure time in Bucharest's parks is not just for the day. Enchanting nighttime experiences can be had in some of these green areas. For example, the promenades around the lake at Herastrău Park are exquisitely lit, resulting in a charming atmosphere ideal for strolls in the evening.

The parks within the city serve as more than just leisure destinations; they are live examples of how important green spaces are in urban settings. They provide chances for social interactions with family and friends as well as time for introspection and isolation. These green spaces serve as a vital counterweight to Bucharest's urban vitality and serve as a reminder to both locals and tourists of the value of getting outside and spending time in nature right in the middle of the city.

The parks and green areas of Bucharest are more than just picturesque scenery; they form an integral part of the city's social fabric. They are locations for rest, discovery, rebirth, and cultural enrichment. Bucharest's parks provide a variety of experiences that appeal to everyone who finds comfort in the embrace of nature, whether you're looking for a leisurely stroll down a tree-lined boulevard, a picnic by a lake, or a moment of peace amid the bustle of the city.

Stroll through Herastrau Park and visit the Village Museum

Herastrau Park is a green haven in the center of Bucharest that provides a peaceful diversion from the bustle of the city. This vast park, which includes Lake Herastrau, is frequently compared to New York City's Central Park. It is a location where leisure, discovering new cultures, and the beauty of nature all coexist peacefully.

All of the senses are stimulated during a leisurely walk in Herastrau Park. A symphony of rustling leaves and birdsong greets you as you enter its pathways lined with trees, providing a calm atmosphere for your exploration. The earthy scent of the park's vegetation fills the air, and the sun dances across the trails ahead, creating a calming interplay of light and shadow.

The broad avenues of the park are ideal for strolling, running, or just finding a peaceful bench to sit on and watch the world go by. Paddleboats can be seen leisurely gliding over the water as you stroll around Lake Herastrau's promenade, which is embellished with picturesque vistas. It's a location where guests can get lost in the calming sounds of the park's natural landscape.

The diversity of gardens and scenery seen inside Herastrau Park's borders is one of its distinguishing qualities. The park displays horticultural expertise in everything from peaceful rose gardens to well-manicured flower beds in full bloom. The gardens are an explosion of color and texture, and the spring and summertime when the flowers are in bloom make them especially charming. The park features artistic horticulture. The gardens are an explosion of color and complexity, and in the spring and summer, when the blossoms are at their best, they are especially mesmerizing.

Herastrau Park is a children's and family's paradise. Thoughtfully positioned around the park are playgrounds and leisure areas that provide kids a chance to run off steam and enjoy some outside time. On the verdant lawns of the park, families frequently meet together for picnics, fostering a sense of belonging and community.

The Village Museum (Muzeul Satului) is an additional addition to the park's cultural value. Nestled in the center of Herastrau Park, this outdoor museum offers a glimpse into the customs and way of life of rural Romania. The museum is a living example of real rural houses and buildings from around the nation. You are taken back in time to a period when rural villages flourished and their architectural traditions became ingrained as you strolled along their paths.

Every home at the Village Museum is a representation of the architectural design, building methods, and cultural legacy of a particular area. Discover everything from little Moldavian cottages to formidable Transylvanian homes. These preserved buildings serve as windows into customs, daily life, and cultural legacies, in addition to serving as displays of architectural diversity.

They offer glimpses into Romania's traditions, way of life, and cultural heritage.

Craftspeople and interpreters in traditional garb bring the Village Museum to life by showcasing a variety of crafts and customs. Blacksmiths hammering iron, weavers crafting elaborate textiles, and potters sculpting clay containers are commonplace. The museum's live history component adds to its vibrancy and interest.

The cooperation between the Village Museum and Herastrau Park is a symbol of Bucharest's commitment to protecting its natural heritage. The park is more than simply a spot to unwind; it's a dynamic landscape that combines history, art, and the natural world to create an immersive experience that enthralls the senses and the intellect.

A walk in Herastrau Park and a visit to the Village Museum offer visitors a chance to delve into the complex layers of Bucharest's cultural identity. Traveling there transports you from the peace and quiet of the natural world to a working museum showcasing the history of rural

America. Combining these two experiences deepens our awareness of Romania's past and shows how history and culture may live side by side in a contemporary city. It's a request to appreciate the present while embracing history and taking in the splendor of Herastrau Park.

Wander through Herastrau Park and the Village Museum, and you'll observe how the natural and cultural worlds interact in a fascinating way. The rich vegetation of the park acts as a gentle reminder of the close relationship that exists between people and the environment. The serene atmosphere of the park promotes reflection and introspection, which deepens awareness of the value of protecting wildlife in urban environments.

Conversely, the Village Museum invites guests to interact with Romania's rich cultural legacy. Every home in the museum serves as a living example of artistic craftsmanship and rural customs. The hardworking guides and craftspeople who breathe life into these buildings are essential in teaching tourists about the traditions, abilities, and inventiveness of the past. A museum is a living, breathing representation of a country's cultural heritage, not just a static display of history.

When combined, Herastrau Park and the Village Museum provide a culturally engaging experience that goes beyond typical museum visits. In an engaging and instructive manner, the museum's outdoor environment, tucked away in the park, encourages visitors to discover and engage with history.

The trip across these areas as a whole also emphasizes Bucharest's dynamic character, which combines the natural and the cultural, as well as the historical and modern. Bucharest is a busy metropolis, but the parks and museums serve as a constant reminder that the city also cherishes its cultural legacy and is dedicated to keeping it alive and presenting it to the rest of the world.

There is no denying the attraction of the Village Museum and Herastrau Park.

These locations offer an enduring allure, whether you're taking a leisurely stroll beneath the trees' canopy, taking in the gardens' riot of colors, or discovering Romania's rich cultural tapestry through its rural structures. These are locations where the past and present coexist, serving as a constant reminder of the intricate relationships between culture, heritage, and the environment, as well as the rich fabric of human history. A trip to these locations is more than simply an outing; it's an exploration of Bucharest's heart and soul, a city where culture and environment coexist in a perfect dance that both enchants and teaches.

Explore Carol Park and the National Military Museum

Carol Park, often called "Parcul Carol," is a culturally, historically, and aesthetically significant location in Bucharest. Situated in the southern region of the city, it provides a diverse experience that combines leisure, discovery, and an opportunity to learn more about Romania's military past.

The park was originally intended to be a public green area in the early 20th century, following the then-popular landscape architectural ideas. Wide alleyways with rows of trees and wonderfully designed flower beds greet you as soon as you reach the park. It is impossible to miss Carol Park's majesty, which reflects its historical origins in symmetry and beauty. that reflect its ancestry in history.

The remarkable architectural tribute to the first Romanian king, the Mausoleum of Carol I, is located in the center of the park. The neoclassical architecture of the mausoleum, with its colonnades and imposing stairway, lends the park's scenery a sense of grandeur. It is a symbol of Bucharest's architectural history as well as a monument to King Carol I. It is also a symbol of the architectural history of Bucharest.

The panoramic viewpoint of Carol Park, which provides amazing views of the city, is one of its most notable attractions. Thanks to its elevated position, tourists may enjoy a great view of Bucharest's diverse architectural landscape, which includes notable buildings like the Palace of the Parliament, which is visible in the distance.

Carol Park is a hub for historical remembrance in addition to being an attractive destination. One of the most important military history-focused organizations in Romania, the National Military Museum (Muzeul Militar Naţional), is located on its premises. The goal of the museum is to conserve and present the nation's military history, spanning from prehistoric periods to contemporary hostilities.

A trip through Romanian history can be had by visiting the National Military Museum. A staggering variety of military relics, from uniforms and weaponry to paperwork and mementos, are on display. It is a location where you can follow the development of the country's armed forces, from the early wars of independence to their participation in the two World Wars and current peacekeeping operations.

The Hall of Merger, which honors Transylvania's 1918 merger with Romania, is one of the museum's centerpieces. The extensive World War I and World War II exhibits at the museum help visitors gain a clearer knowledge of Romania's experiences throughout two major international conflicts.

The National Military Museum frequently holds temporary exhibitions and educational events in addition to its collection of historical items. These occasions give us a window into different facets of military history and give us a chance to think and learn.

Bucharest's dedication to cultural and historical preservation is reflected in the collaboration between Carol Park and the National Military Museum. It's a location where historical lessons and urban park beauty coexist together. The park's and museum's historical significance serves as a reminder of the country's bravery, hardships, and historical contributions to the world.

Discovering Carol Park and the National Military Museum is an experience that delves deeply into Bucharest's past and rich cultural legacy, surpassing mere sightseeing. It's a chance to recognize how dedicated the city is to maintaining its history while still embracing the changes of the modern era. Carol Park is a site of respect, leisure, and introspection where the teachings of The natural beauty of the world finds a place for history.

You'll discover that the National Military Museum in Carol Park provides a chance for introspection and a link to the history of the country as you explore more. The items on show, which include anything from military gear and uniforms to soldier diaries and private letters, offer a glimpse into the struggles and sacrifices made by people who have molded Romania's identity.

The museum recognizes the value of citizen initiatives and resiliency during times of conflict, in addition to the valor displayed by troops on the battlefield. This thorough method of narrating Romania's military history emphasizes the nation's spirit and emphasizes that towns, families, and individuals all played significant roles in addition to the soldiers.

The World War II exhibit in the museum is among its most impactful displays. This is a crucial historical moment for

Romania. This section examines the difficulties the nation encountered during the conflict as well as the difficult military and political choices it made. The museum presents a complex analysis of this period of history, giving visitors the chance to reflect on the decisions By providing a fair assessment of this historical era, the museum allows visitors to consider the choices and challenges that defined that time in history.

The museum routinely hosts events, lectures, and educational activities, making it a lively space for learning and conversation. Academics, historians, and the general public are brought together to establish a platform where history is actively analyzed and discussed instead of just being told.

The National Military Museum and Carol Park, with their verdant surroundings and calm atmosphere, are placed next to one another to emphasize the cohabitation of historical significance and beauty. This place blends art and education so that guests can take in the grace of a city park and explore history in a meaningful way.

Carol Park and the National Military Museum serve as more than just cultural hubs for locals and visitors—they are places of contemplation and remembering. They serve as a reminder of the value of remembering the past, appreciating the sacrifices made for the present, and preserving history.

Ultimately, a visit to Carol Park and the National Military Museum in Bucharest is a celebration of the perseverance and tenacity of a country, not only a trip through time. It is evidence of a city's capacity to honor its history while anticipating a future influenced by the knowledge gained from the past. Visiting these locations offers a chance to engage with Romania's collective memory and recognize the influence of history and the environment on the country's cultural identity.

Experience the vibrant nightlife in Bucharest.

The nightlife of Bucharest is a colorful tapestry made of many different hues, sounds, and tastes. After dark, the capital of Romania comes to life with a wide range of events to suit every taste and desire. Bucharest offers a diverse range of experiences for all types of travelers, including small jazz bars, throbbing sounds on the dance floor, and tranquil evenings in evocative pubs.

A famous part of Bucharest's nightlife is the Old Town, or "Lipscani." When the sun goes down, this historic quarter becomes a hive of activity. Numerous establishments, including hipster-friendly cocktail bars, vibrant nightclubs, and traditional Romanian eateries, may be found along the winding cobblestone streets. You may hear live music reverberating from establishments as you go throughout this area, and the moody lighting gives the scene a cozy, inviting light.

The wide variety of music venues in Bucharest is one of its unique features. There are small jazz clubs for people who enjoy the genre where excellent performers provide the ideal atmosphere for a restful evening. Jazz lovers will enjoy the lovely experience of seeing both local and international artists perform in these quaint locations.

Bucharest has a thriving party scene for those who enjoy dancing to electronic music. The city is renowned for producing some of the best electronic music producers and DJs. The clubs frequently feature both domestic and foreign performers, resulting in a lively scene on the dance floors that extends far into the wee hours of the morning. Whether you're into mainstream music or underground techno, you may find a club that appeals to you because each one has its own ambiance.

Bucharest's nightlife also heavily relies on the city's clubs and pubs. Breweries and pubs are offering a large assortment of locally brewed beers, which is contributing to the growing popularity of craft beer. These locations are ideal for a more carefree and informal evening, where you can sip fine drinks and strike up discussions with nearby residents and other tourists.

In addition, during the summer months, Bucharest hosts outdoor concerts and festivals as part of its vibrant nightlife. Music festivals and cultural events are held in parks, squares, and historic sites, drawing people from all across the nation and beyond. These outdoor events, where music, art, and culture converge under the starry sky, foster a feeling of community and celebration.

The nightlife in Bucharest also has an element of surprise and uncertainty. The tapestry includes underground parties, pop-up events, and hidden gem locations. These adventures add a dash of adventure to your nights out and are typically found by word of mouth or by interacting with the local population. incorporating some adventure into your get-togethers.

Ultimately, Bucharest's nighttime culture is intrinsically linked to the essence of the city. It is a location where conversations flow, where cultures collide, and where dance floors serve as platforms for individual expression. You have the chance to fully immerse yourself in the sounds and rhythms of a city that never really sleeps, where the days and nights are equally colorful, and where you can make experiences that will last long after your trip.

Essentially, becoming a part of Bucharest's lively nightlife is an invitation to discover the spirit of the city after dark. It's a chance to feel the pulse of the city, find hidden treasures, and engage with the vibrant and diverse vibe of Romania's capital. Bucharest's nightlife is more than just a series of events; it's a vivid representation of the cultural richness of the city and living evidence of its lively heart.

Printed in Great Britain
by Amazon